# The
# BASIC Conversions
# Handbook for
# APPLE™, TRS-80™,
# and PET™ Users

# The BASIC Conversions Handbook for APPLE™, TRS-80™, and PET™ Users

## BRAIN BANK

David A. Brain, Philip R. Oviate,
Paul J. A. Paquin, and Chandler D. Stone, Jr.

HAYDEN BOOK COMPANY, INC.
Rochelle Park, New Jersey

**Library of Congress Catologing in Publication Data**

Main entry under title:

The BASIC conversions handbook for APPLE, TRS-80, and
  PET users.

  1. Basic (Computer program language)  2. Apple
computer—Programming.  3. TRS-80 (Computer)—Pro-
gramming.  4. PET (Computer)—Programming.  I. Brain,
David A.  II. Brain Bank (Firm)
QA76.73.B3B39        001.64'24        81-6898
ISBN 0-8104-5534-X                    AACR2

TRS-80 is a trademark of Radio Shack, a Division of Tandy Corporation, and is not affiliated with Hayden Book Co., Inc.

Apple is a trademark of Apple Computer Co., Inc., and is not affiliated with Hayden Book Co., Inc.

PET is a trademark of Commodore Business Machines, Inc., and is not affiliated with Hayden Book Co., Inc.

*Printed in the United States of America*

6  7  8  9   PRINTING

83  84  85  86  87  88  89    YEAR

# Preface

After purchasing my first computer and spending many hours programming and learning how to make it work, I began writing programs for specific applications.

I realized very quickly that a lot of the programs I needed were already written, but many of them were in various other BASIC languages. It was also obvious not only that BASIC differs from machine to machine but also that each machine might have different versions of their own BASIC (for example, Level I and Level II, Integer and APPLESOFT II)!

With the help of a good friend who owned a different machine, we began to explore the differences between the languages. After a lot of research we found that, even though many commands were different, for the most part they performed similar functions (for example, the command CLS in TRS-80 does exactly the same thing as the command HOME in APPLE II).

As a result of our explorations on many different machines, we put together this guide to help translate programs into a variety of machine "languages." With this guide you will be able to select a program in its listed form and translate it to your particular machine, thus saving you from having to "reinvent the wheel."

There are a few considerations that must be kept in mind while you are translating. First, since the video formats differ from machine to machine, you will have to adjust print statements for the size of the video on your machine. Second, each machine has its own particular graphics capabilities, and, although graphics are discussed briefly in the various chapters, your own imagination will be your best guide to the kind of graphics you will want to use. Third, we have found through experience that most errors occur in our translations as a result of the incorrect formatting of IF . . . THEN statements. Since every machine has its own peculiarities concerning

IF ... THEN statements, you should take extra care to understand the purpose of these statements and their desired results.

We sincerely hope that this guide will allow you to make better use of your equipment and save you trouble in translating by providing a quick reference to the mysteries of those "other machines."

A lot of effort and time went into the compiling of this book, and its completion was due largely to the patience of Pat and Jane.

D. A. BRAIN

# Contents

# Chapter 1
# METHODS
# OF TRANSLATION

With the advent of the microcomputer, accessibility to computer technology has increased enormously. Prices are now within the reach of most individuals, and the software support is increasing almost daily.

The major problem in the field of microcomputing today, however, is still software support. The number and variety of programs available to microcomputer owners are virtually infinite, but the types of software available are very limited. This situation has come about for a number of reasons, not the least of which is marketability. If a program does not appear to have a very wide appeal, it will probably not be published on tape or disk for the consumer. A large variety of programs is available, however, in the various magazines for the microcomputing market. It is to these listed programs that we will address our efforts.

The published programs themselves often create another problem. If the program is one that we might want to use, it may or may not be in the correct machine language for us to use it. Each computer has its own strong and weak points, but the major problem is that none of the available languages are compatible (we are able, however, to make the machines compatible). For whatever reason, each manufacturer has its own version of BASIC that runs only on its own machine.

Fortunately, software follows the same sort of logic no matter what brand of machine it is written on. Programs written for one microcomputer will work on just about any other kind if the language differences are compensated for.

The BASIC (Beginner's All-purpose Symbolic Instruction Code) language has been accepted as more-or-less standard for almost all microcomputers, but each manufacturer has added (or left out) a few commands or used different labels (or commands) to perform the same function (the command CLS in TRS-80, the command HOME in APPLE II, and the command PRINT"⬜" in PET all do the same thing). Fortunately, there is enough similarity between machines to allow us to translate programs from one machine to another.

In this book, we will consider three of the most popular microcomputers on the market (TRS-80, APPLE II, and PET) and show how you can translate programs for one machine for use on the machine available to you.

When preparing to use a listing made for another machine, you will save a lot of time if you sit down with the listing and try to figure out the flow of the program before starting to translate it. There may be improvements you can make based on your own experience, or you may find specific commands that need subroutines for which you will have to allow additional space. Having an understanding of how the program works will not only speed up the process of translation but also help you format your screen display. Differences in some of the functions of the various machines will create problems if you don't plan ahead and identify them in advance.

The major differences you will encounter are in the area of graphics. Different machines have different graphic capabilities, and any attempt to "translate" will result in extreme frustration. The best course of action is to determine exactly what it is that should be graphically displayed, refer to the screen charts at the back of the book, and use your imagination to create your own graphics. I look upon this part of translating as a challenge, and it usually turns out to be the most interesting part of the program.

Some of the programs you encounter will present problems that are not covered in this book. The most common problem will occur in programs or subroutines written in machine language. Machine-language routines are used primarily to save memory and speed up the execution of a program. Usually, if you understand the flow of a program, you will be able to determine what the machine-language routine is supposed to do. If so, you can probably create a BASIC subroutine to accomplish the same result.

This book has been organized in three major chapters. Each of these deals with a specific machine, and each major section of each chapter deals with one given language. Some of the functions described are provided for background information only. In each section all the commands you are likely to encounter in a program listing are compared to instructions used on your own machine. The basic format for this guide is:

| *Listing Command* | *Your Machine Command* | *Comments* |

Any peculiarities of a machine are listed at the end of each section.

Here is a simple example of how a translation is made from the TRS-80 to APPLESOFT II. Suppose that the program listing in the TRS-80 is

```
10   CLS : PRINT "HELLO" : END
```

Refer to Sec. 3.1 of Chap. 3 to find the equivalent command to CLS in APPLESOFT II . It appears as follows:

|  CLS  |  HOME |

In your program converting TRS-80 to APPLESOFT II, you would therefore type:

```
10   HOME :
```

Then, in case you aren't sure, look up the commands END and PRINT in the same way. After the line has been completely translated, it will look like this:

```
10   HOME : PRINT "HELLO" : END
```

After studying this book and translating a few programs, you will soon recognize what needs to be changed and what can remain the same.

In case you should need a quick guide to what some of the commands mean, a detailed explanation of APPLE II commands has been provided in the section for translation of APPLE II to TRS-80. Although the intent of the author is not to teach you how to program, this quick reference source may help you if you should come across an unfamiliar command while doing your translation.

Ultimately, the purpose of this book is to expand your access to a much larger variety of software so that you can choose the kind best suited to your needs.

# Chapter 2

# CONVERSION OF APPLE II AND PET PROGRAMS INTO TRS-80

This chapter is designed for easy conversion of PET and APPLE II programs into TRS-80. On the whole, the commands are in alphabetical order for quick reference. Several subroutines are included to allow you to approximate PET or APPLE II commands that do not directly relate to TRS-80 commands.

Graphics will again be discussed from the standpoint of what can and what cannot be done, but, for the most part, your own imagination will be the best guide in trying to convert APPLE II and PET graphics into TRS-80.

The format for this chapter is as follows:

| APPLE II/PET Function | TRS-80 Function | Comments |
|---|---|---|

Every command with a direct relationship to TRS-80 is included, but a few TRS-80 commands that do not relate to either the PET or APPLE II are not listed. Subroutines and other conversion considerations that allow the TRS-80 to perform a PET or APPLE II function will be found in the comments section at the side of each command.

## Notes on TRS-80 Model III

TRS-80 Model III has all the language features of Model I and a few more. The addresses—PEEKS and POKES (see the list below)—are different in some cases, of course, but, for the most part, Model I and III are very similar.

Although there have been hardware modifications, these will not alter the translation of listed programs. Video display addresses and graphics characters (128–191) are identical. In fact, from a translation standpoint, Model I and Model III BASIC are identical except for the addition of TIME$, which relates to the real-time clock.

The video display of Model III uses a different character set: an additional set of 96 special characters.

Although some Model I software will not run on Model III, you will still be able to translate the listings by using the guide to Model I.

The POKES in Model III are as follows:

| | |
|---|---|
| 16412,1 | Set blinking or solid cursor; can be eliminated |
| 16419,176 | Code for cursor character is in this location; can be eliminated |
| 16916,x | Affects scrolling of x lines of screen; can be eliminated |
| 16888 | Serial I/O baud rate code |
| 16890 | Serial I/O Wait/Don't Wait switch |
| 16872 | Character input buffer |
| 16880 | Character output buffer |
| 16889 | Parity/Word length/Stop bit |
| 16928 to 16931 | SOURCE and DESTINATION memory locations; can be eliminated |
| 16919 to 16924 | Real-Time clock; can be eliminated |

## 2.1 Conversion of APPLE II into TRS-80

### Commands

| APPLE II | TRS-80 | Comments |
| --- | --- | --- |
| ABS(x) | ABS(x) | Same function. The command ABS (variable) returns the absolute value of the variable x. The command is valid in Integer and Floating-Point BASIC. |
| AND | AND | Same function. AND is a logical operator. When it is used in an assertion, both elements of the statement on either side of the AND must be true, or the entire statement will be viewed by the computer as false. AND is used in both Integer and Floating-Point BASIC. |
| ASC("x") or ASC(x) | ASC(x) | Same function. The command ASC(variable) returns the decimal equivalent of standard ASCII code. The operation is valid in Integer and Floating-Point BASIC. In Integer BASIC programs, the "x" may or may not be seen. The quotation marks perform no additional function. |
| ATN(x) | ATN(x) | Same function. The command ATN(variable) returns a value for the variable or a number expressed in radians. The ATN(variable) function is not available in Level I. |
| AUTO xxx | AUTO xxx | Same function. The command produces automatic line numbering, in which xxx specifies the starting line number. If no increment is |

**Commands** *(continued)*

| APPLE II | TRS-80 | Comments |
|---|---|---|
| | | entered, the machine will increment each line number by 10. AUTO line numbering is not available in Level I. |
| AUTO xxx,yy | AUTO xxx,yy | Same function. The command produces automatic line numbering in which xxx designates the starting line number and yy the increment by which the line numbers will increase. |
| CHR$(7) | None | In an APPLE II program, CHR$(7) will cause the computer's built-in speaker to "beep." There is no direct equivalent operation available to the TRS-80 without modification. In a conversion, it is not necessary to include the function. |
| CALL x | USR(∅) | Partially similar function. On APPLE II, the CALL expression will cause the computer to execute a machine-language subroutine beginning at the memory address specified by the expression. There is no equivalent available to Level I. In Level II, the function can be approximated as follows: |
| | | POKE 16526,y: POKE 16527,z: x=USR(∅) |
| | | (Note: y designates the most significant byte and z designates the least significant. See USR command in Level II manual.) |

| | | |
|---|---|---|
| CHR$(x) | CHR$(x) | Same function. CHR$(variable) returns the ASCII equivalent of the decimal within the parentheses. The function is not available in Level I. |
| CLEAR | CLEAR | Approximately the same function. On APPLE II, CLEAR sets all variables to zero and all strings to null (" "). In Level II, it may be necessary to execute a CLEAR xxx, where xxx indicates the amount of string space to be reserved. |
| CLR | CLEAR | Same function as described above. CLR is found in Integer BASIC programs. Note that it is not necessary for the APPLE II to reserve string space as this function is performed automatically by the computer. |
| COLOR=x | None | In all APPLE II graphics, a color must be specified prior to attempting to plot a point or line. In Integer BASIC, x will equal any number from $\emptyset$ to 15 and will usually be preceded by the command GR. In Floating-Point BASIC, x will equal $\emptyset$ to 15 (following the command GR:) or $\emptyset$ to 7 (following the command HGR:). On the TRS-80, no color graphics function is currently available without modification, and hence the command can be ignored. |
| CON | CONT | Same function. The command causes the program to continue its operation where it was stopped. Variables are not reset. |

**Commands** *(continued)*

| APPLE II | TRS-80 | Comments |
|----------|--------|----------|
| CONT | CONT | Same function as described above. The command will be found in Floating-Point BASIC. |
| COS(x) | COS(x) | Same function. The COS(variable) command returns the cosine of the variable x. This function is not available in Level I. |
| DATAx,y,z | DATAx,y,z | Same function. When a READ command is encountered in a program, DATAx,y,z will be read sequentially. |
| DIMx(y) | DIMx(y) | Same function. When a DIMx(y) command is executed, the computer will set aside y spaces for an x array of variables. |
| DIMx$(y) | DIMx$(y) | Same function. When a DIMx$(y) command is executed the computer will set aside y dimensions for an array of x$ variables. |
| DEF FN x | None | This command in an APPLE II program allows the programmer to define a function and then utilize that function again by using the command FN x. Since there is no equivalent TRS-80 command, it must be specified each time it is needed. |
| DEL x | DELETE x | Same function. The command DEL x causes the line number x to be deleted from the program. |
| DEL x,y | DELETE x-y | Same function. The command deletes all line numbers between (and including) x and y from the program. |

| | | |
|---|---|---|
| DRAW x | None | When encountered in a Floating-Point BASIC program, the computer will draw shape number x (previously loaded in machine language) at the next point identified; for example, DRAW x AT y. There is no equivalent function available in the TRS-80. However POKE graphics may be used as an approximate substitute. (See Level II manual.) |
| END | END | Same function. In all cases, the command END will terminate the execution of a program whenever encountered. |
| EXP(x) | EXP(x) | Same function. The command EXP(x) will raise a variable to the indicated power x. This function is available in Level II only. |
| FOR x=y TO z: NEXT | FOR x=y TO z: NEXT | Same function (a common loop). In Level I, NEXT must be followed by the specified variable. (Example: FOR x=y TO z: NEXT x). When the function is used as a timing loop, it should be remembered that the APPLE II operates approximately two and a half times faster than the TRS-80. Timing loops should be reduced by a factor of 2.5. |
| FLASH | None | The command FLASH causes everything printed (displayed) on the screen to FLASH. Although there is no directly related TRS-80 command, one way to approximate the function is as follows:<br><br>FOR X=1 TO 20: PRINT @ 936, "HELLO":<br>FOR y=1 TO 50: NEXT Y: PRINT @ 936, "     ": NEXT X |

## Commands *(continued)*

| APPLE II | TRS-80 | Comments |
|---|---|---|
| FRE(x) | FRE(x) | Approximately same function. The command FRE(x) returns the amount of memory available to the user. It also serves to houseclean the computer of miscellaneous data that has no function within a current program. |
| GET x$ | INKEY$ | Similar function. The common GET (variable)$ causes the program to halt and wait for a string variable x to be input. It is not necessary for the ENTER key to be pressed for the input to be accepted. INKEY$ does not cause program flow to halt. You must force it to wait by means of the following: |
| | | 1Ø  IF INKEY$=" " THEN GOTO 1Ø |
| | | The APPLE II command GET x$ need not be followed by the evaluation and limiting statements needed on the TRS-80. |
| GOSUB x | GOSUB x | Same function. The branching statement GOSUB (line number) sends the program operation to the subroutine located at the line number specified. The next RETURN command encountered will return the flow of operation to the place in the program where the GOSUB was encountered. |
| GOTO x | GOTO x | Same function. The branching statement GOTO (line number) will send the program operation to the line number specified. |

| | | |
|---|---|---|
| GR | None | No equivalent function is needed on the TRS-80. The GR command on the APPLE II is needed to switch the screen display to the LO-RES graphics mode, whose screen is normally a 40 by 40 matrix. (See Appendix C for screen conversion.) |
| HCOLOR=x | None | No equivalent function exists on the TRS-80 without modification. The command is needed on the APPLE II following the HGR command to designate which of the seven HGR colors will be used. A color value (∅ to 7) will be designated. For the purposes of conversion, this command and its elements should be ignored. |
| HGR or HGR2 | None | No equivalent function exists on the TRS-80 or is necessary for conversion. The HGR command on the APPLE II sets the screen to the HI-RES graphics mode. HI-RES graphics are not available on the TRS-80 without modification. The closest TRS-80 procedure available may be the use of POKE graphics (Level II only), which will approximate the desired display. (See Level II manual.) |
| HIMEM=x | MEMORY SIZE ? | Same function |
| HLIN x,y AT z | None | The command HLIN is a graphics-related command. It draws a horizontal line from x to y at the vertical position z on the screen. It may be approximated as follows:

FOR z=x TO y; SET(Z,Y): NEXTZ |

**Commands** *(continued)*

| APPLE II | TRS-80 | Comments |
|---|---|---|
| | | This will draw a line from x to y at the vertical position Y(z). |
| HOME | CLS | Same function. This command clears the display screen and returns the cursor to the upper left corner of the screen. |
| HPLOT x,y | None | This command is the HI-RES graphic equivalent of SET (x,y). No equivalent exists on the TRS-80 without modification. ASCII characters may sometimes be POKED on the screen to approximate the desired results. The TRS-80 command PRINT @ may also serve as an adequate substitute. |
| HTAB x<br>or<br>HTAB (x) | PRINT @<br>or<br>TAB(x) | On the APPLE II, HTAB x will move the cursor (and next print location) horizontally to position x of the print line that is currently being displayed. |
| IF . . . . THEN | IF . . . THEN | Same function. IF . . . THEN is a conditional control statement. In a Floating-Point BASIC program, all commands after this statement will be ignored if the statement is false. In an Integer BASIC program, the statement functions in the same way it does on the TRS-80. |
| IN# x | None | This command addresses a peripheral slot within the APPLE II designated by x. On a TRS-80, no equivalent exists without an expansion interface and associated equipment. |

Depending on the data being transferred to the computer by the command, it may be possible to approximate the function by the use of the INPUT#-x command and an attached cassette recorder. (See the TRS-80 manual.)

| | | |
|---|---|---|
| INPUT". . . ." | INPUT". . . ." | Same function. Program operation will halt until the requested data is entered in the computer. The command will print whatever is between the quotation marks on the screen and put a ? and cursor after it. |
| INPUT x | INPUT x | Same function. The program operation will halt and wait for the requested simple variable to be entered. |
| INPUT x,y,z | INPUT x,y,z | Same function. The program operation will halt until each of the simple variables has been entered. The variables must be numbers only. |
| INPUT A$ | INPUT A$ | Same function. The program execution will halt until the requested string variable is entered. Note that TRS-80 Level I will accept only two string variables: A$ and B$. |
| INT(x) | INT(x) | Same function. The command INT(x) will return the integer of the variable x. In converting some Integer BASIC programs to TRS-80, it may be necessary to check any division performed. Since APPLE II Integer BASIC will automatically return an integer, it may be necessary to insert an INT(x) in a TRS-80 conversion. |

## Commands *(continued)*

| APPLE II | TRS-80 | Comments |
|----------|--------|----------|
| INVERSE | None | No equivalent command exists on the TRS-80 for this command, which causes any text printed under it to be displayed as black letters on a white background. Conversion is not needed. |
| LEFT$(X$,x) | LEFT$(X$,x) | Same function in Level II but not available in Level I. This command causes the computer to recognize (or operate on) x number of characters of X$, starting from the left side of the string. |
| LEN(X$) | LEN(X$) | Same function. The command LEN(X$) will return a numeric that equals the number of characters within X$. This function is not available in TRS-80 Level I. |
| LET | LET | Same function. This optional command may be encountered when a simple variable is set equal to some other simple variable. It is not necessary to include it in a conversion. |
| LIST | LIST | Same function. The command LIST will cause the entire program to be listed sequentially by line number from beginning to end. |
| LIST x<br>LIST x,y<br>LIST x-y<br>LIST x-<br>LIST, x | LIST x<br>LIST x-y<br>LIST x-y<br>LIST x-<br>LIST=x | Same function. LIST x will display the line number designated by x. LIST x,y will display line numbers x through y as will LIST x-y. LIST x- will display from line number x to the end of the program. |

| | | |
|---|---|---|
| LOAD | CLOAD | Same function. The command LOAD causes the computer to accept incoming data from the tape cassette player. Execution of this command may be immediate or deferred. |
| LOG(x) | LOG(x) | Same function. LOG(expression) will return the natural logarithm of the expression. This function is not available in Level I. |
| LOMEM | None | No equivalent function is available in the TRS-80. Since LOMEM is used in APPLE II programs to prevent HI-RES graphics from clobbering the variable storage area of the memory, it is not usually required in a conversion. |
| MID$(".....", y,z) or MID$(X$,y,z) | MID$(".....", y,z) or MID$(X$,y,z) | Same function. In both cases, the command will cause the computer to read the string starting with the y character designated and read the z characters indicated. This function is not available in Level I. |
| NEW | NEW | Same function. Execution of the command (either immediate or deferred) sets all program pointers to the machine basic program start point and effectually deletes the current program and all previous variables. |
| NEXT | NEXT | Same function. The command NEXT indicates the "bottom" of a FOR . . . NEXT loop. Depending on the Level (I or II), it may be necessary to specify what variable is NEXT (for example, NEXT x). |

**Commands** *(continued)*

| APPLE II | TRS-80 | Comments |
|---|---|---|
| NORMAL | None | No equivalent function exists or is needed on the TRS-80. The command terminates the operation of the APPLE II commands FLASH and INVERSE. |
| NOT | NOT | Same function. The logical operator NOT is usually found in a statement that may include an IF or an AND (see TRS-80 Manual). |
| NOTRACE | TROFF | Same function. Although not commonly used in programs, this command turns off the line number TRACE function of the computer. |
| ON ERR GOTO | ON ERROR GOTO | Same function. This command may be inserted in a program if an error is likely to occur at a given point. In a Floating-Point BASIC program, one might also find a POKE 216,Ø in the proximity of the error-handling statement or whereever the program flow has been sent. This POKE command sets the APPLE II's error-detecting flag back to its normal error-handling operation. |
| ON x GOSUB xx,yy,zz | ON x GOSUB xx,yy,zz | Same function. Each increment of x encountered will cause a branch to the subroutine at its corresponding line number, execute the subroutine, and return to its point of departure within the program. |
| ON x GOTO xx,yy,zz | ON x GOTO xx,yy,zz | Same function. Each increment of x encountered will cause a branch to its equivalent or specified corresponding line number. |

|  |  | Program operation will continue from the line number designated. |
|---|---|---|
| OR | OR | Same function. OR is a logical operator used in a comparison or relationship. |
| PDL(x) | None | The PDL(x) function is not available in the TRS-80 without modification. PDL refers to the game controllers that are available on APPLE II computers. The (x) will normally be a value between Ø and 3, indicating which of the controls is to be read. |
| PEEK(x) | PEEK(x) | Same function. It returns the decimal equivalent of the contents of the memory address specified by (x). This function is not available in Level I. |
| PLOT x,y | SET(x,y) | Same function. On APPLE II, the command PLOT will turn on a LO-RES graphics block specified by the variables x and y or any expression used to produce a number within the limits of the screen. |
| POKE x,y | POKE x,y | Same function. It stores the machine-language equivalent of the variable y at memory address x. POKE is not available to Level I. |
| POS(Ø) | POS(Ø) | Same function. POS(Ø) will return the horizontal position value (Ø to the length of the TAB field) of the current cursor location. |
| PR#x | None | On APPLE II this command sends computer output to the peripheral slot designated by x. No direct TRS-80 equivalent exists without the expansion interface and associated peripheral hardware. In some cases |

## Commands *(continued)*

| *APPLE II* | *TRS-80* | *Comments* |
|---|---|---|
| | | it may be possible to address the output to the cassette recorder with the PRINT#-1 command. |
| PRINT | PRINT | Same function. This command causes the specified operation to be displayed on the video screen. |
| READ x | READ x | Same function. The command READ will cause the variable indicated (x) to accept the successive values as they occur in the programs DATA statements. The command may also be followed by a string designator (READ X$). This will cause all the DATA statement elements to be read as strings. Reading strings is not available on Level I. |
| RECALL x | INPUT#-1 | Approximately the same function. In APPLE II programs, the command will cause the computer to input data from the cassette recorder. The data will be in the form of simple numerical variables or a real or integer array. Data "recalled" will be stored in a previously dimensioned array or variable list. |
| REM | REM | Same function. The command REM allows the programmer to include nonoperational text in the program as remarks. REM statements may be included or ignored. If a REM is left out, be sure that nothing in the program branches to the line number excluded. |
| RESTORE | RESTORE | Same function. The command RESTORE causes the stack pointer |

| | | |
|---|---|---|
| | | of the data list to reset to the beginning of the program's DATA lines. The next READ command encountered will cause DATA to be read from the beginning of the list. |
| RETURN | RETURN | Same function. RETURN will complete the branching statement initiated by the command GOSUB. Program operation will return to the location where the GOSUB was encountered and begin with the next command or operation (see POP). |
| RESUME | RESUME | Usually the same function. This command at the end of an error-handling routine (ONERR GOTO) will cause the program operation to continue from the point where the error occurred. All previous variables remain in memory except for those that may have been part of the original error. |
| RIGHT$(X$,y) or RIGHT$(". . .", y) | RIGHT$(X$,y) or RIGHT$(". . .", y) | Same function. This command will cause the computer to read the designated string (X$) from the right end to the character that is y places from the right. Any action performed will be done on the last y characters of the string. |
| RND (X) | RND(X) | Approximately the same function. RND(X) will return a value between Ø and 1 (.00000001 to .99999999) only, regardless of the value of X. |
| RND (Ø) | RND(Ø) | Same function. RND(Ø) returns the most recently generated random number between Ø and 1. |
| RND(-X) | RANDOM | Same function. This command will generate a specific random number |

**Commands** *(continued)*

| APPLE II | TRS-80 | Comments |
|----------|--------|----------|
| | | that will be the same each time the argument is encountered. Positive RND numbers used in conjunction with the negative RND will vary in a particular, repeatable sequence. Any new RND (positive number) used outside the argument will be treated normally (see Level II manual). |
| ROT | None | No equivalent function exists in the TRS-80. The command ROT is used in conjunction with a HI-RES graphics SHAPE that has been entered in the computer in machine language. Depending on the SHAPE drawn, it may be possible to approximate it with a POKE graphic combination. If so, the shape will have to be re-POKED on the screen to vary its location. |
| RUN | RUN | Same function. The command sets all variables to Ø or " " (null) and directs program execution to start at the lowest line number of the program. |
| RUN x | RUN x | Same function. RUN x will set all variables to Ø or " " (null), but program execution will begin at the line number specified by the number x. |
| SAVE | CSAVE | Same function. This command will cause the computer to store the current program in memory on cassette. |

| | | |
|---|---|---|
| SCALE=x | None | The command SCALE is applied to the commands of DRAW and XDRAW in a Floating-Point BASIC program. SCALE sets the relative size of the machine-language SHAPE to be drawn in HI-RES graphics. No equivalent command is available or needed in the TRS-80. Size will increase from 1 to 255 times. (SCALE=∅ is the largest possible.) To approximate the function, the shape will have to be plotted larger manually or scaled with a subroutine. |
| SCRN(x,y) | POINT(x,y) | Similar function. In the LO-RES graphics mode, SCRN(x,y) will return the value of the color of the graphics block at the point specified by coordinates x,y. |
| SGN(x) | SGN(x) | Same mathematical function. SGN(x) will return the sign (−1, ∅, or 1) of the value of the argument (−1 for negative, ∅ for value of ∅, and 1 for a positive value). |
| SHLOAD | None | No equivalent function. This command loads a HI-RES graphics shape from the cassette to just under the HIMEM limit of the memory. In a Floating-Point BASIC program, HIMEM will then be set below the shape to protect it. The closest approximation available on the TRS-80 may be achieved by saving a simple shape as a DIMension and using the INPUT#-1 (and PRINT#-1) command to retrieve a specific shape. |
| SIN(x) | SIN(x) | Same mathematical function. SIN(x) will return the sine of the number |

| *APPLE II* | *TRS-80* | *Comments* |
|---|---|---|
| | | specified by x. This command is not available to Level I. |
| SPC(x) | STRING$(x,32) | Approximately the same function. In an APPLE II program, SPC(x) will be used in a PRINT statement. The command will cause x number of spaces to be inserted between the last PRINT if followed by a semicolon(;) and the next element to be PRINTed if SPC(x) is followed by a semicolon(;). |
| SPEED=x | None | No equivalent function. The SPEED command in an APPLE II program allows the user to adjust the speed at which characters are displayed on the screen (or peripheral device) from a high of 255 (normal speed) to a low of Ø. To approximate the function, TRS-80 PRINT statements can be slowed down through the use of timing loops and READ-DATA routines where feasible. Otherwise no conversion is available or needed. |
| SQR(x) | SQR(x) | Same mathematical function. SQR(x) returns the square root of the number or expression specified by x. This command is not available to Level I. |
| STEP x | STEP x | Same function. Used within a FOR . . . NEXT loop, the command will cause the program operation to increment (count) through the loop in multiples of x. |

| | | |
|---|---|---|
| STEP −x | STEP −x | Same function. Used within a FOR . . . NEXT loop, the command will cause the program operation to decrement the starting value of x by multiples of x. |
| STOP | STOP | Same function. This command causes the program operation to STOP at the line number where the command is encountered. The computer will display the line number where the program stopped on returning control to the user. |
| STORE x | PRINT#-1 | Generally the same function. The command will write an integer or real array to the cassette. The data stored may then be accessed from a running program by the command INPUT#-1 (RECALL on APPLE II). The handling of data in this manner requires that storage area for the incoming-outgoing data be previously DIMensioned within the program. |
| STR$(x) | STR$(x) | Same function. This command will take the variables or expressions within the parentheses (x) and return them as a string. This function is not available to TRS-80 Level I. |
| TAB(x) | TAB(x) | Same function. TAB(x) will cause the cursor to tab x number of positions to the right of the left-hand margin of the screen. |
| TAN(x) | TAN(x) | Same mathematical function. This command will return the value of the tangent of the argument or expression specified by x, which must be in radians. This function is not available in Level I. |

| APPLE II | TRS-80 | Comments |
|---|---|---|
| TEXT | None | No equivalent function. The TEXT command in APPLE II programs is required to switch from a graphics display mode (both HI-RES and LO-RES) to an all-text mode of display. No similar command is needed in the TRS-80. |
| TRACE | TRON | Same function. The command causes the line number of program operation to be displayed on the screen along with the operation being performed by the computer (see NOTRACE). The TRON feature is not available in Level I. |
| USR(x) | USR(Ø) | Similar function. The command allows the user to place the value of the expression within the parentheses in a specific memory address where it may be accessed by machine-language routines. The machine-language routine must have been previously POKEd or directly entered into the computer (see CALL). This function is not available to Level I. (See also Level II manual.) |
| VAL("xyz") or VAL(X$) | VAL("xyz") or VAL(X$) | Same function. This command will cause the computer to try to evaluate the designated string in numeric terms. It will read the string up to the first nonnumeric character and return the value of the numbers read as a real or integer. If the first characters are letters or nonnumeric symbols, the string will be read as |

having a value of $\emptyset$. This function is not available to Level I.

| | | |
|---|---|---|
| VLIN a,b AT c | None | No direct equivalent exists in the TRS-80. The function draws a vertical line from point a to point b at the horizontal position c. The function can be approximated by the routine:<br><br>FOR y=a TO b: SET(c,y):NEXTy |
| VTAB x<br>or<br>VTAB (x) | PRINT@ x | On the APPLE II, the command VTAB will move the cursor to the horizontal row (or tab vertically) to the position specified by the variable x. On the TRS-80, the PRINT @ command specifying the appropriate left-margin position will duplicate the function well. |
| WAIT<br>    xxxxx,yyy,z<br>or<br>WAIT<br>    xxxxx,yyy | None | No equivalent function exists in the TRS-80. The command WAIT permits the programmer to use a conditional pause within an operating program. The computer will wait until the bit state of the address specified by xxxxx matches the binary equivalent of the decimal number specified by yyy. If a third expression is present (z), it will equal 1 or $\emptyset$. The 1 indicates that you are waiting for the corresponding bit state to be low, $\emptyset$ for the corresponding bit state to be high. ($\emptyset$ is assumed if no third expression is stated.) When the designated conditions are met, the operation will continue. (See APPLESOFT II Basic Programming Reference Manual.) |

| APPLE II | TRS-80 | Comments |
|----------|--------|----------|
| XDRAW z AT x,y | None | This command will draw the same shape previously drawn by the command DRAW z AT x,y in the complement of the COLOR previously used. It has the effect of "erasing" the shape drawn if the background color is the complement of the color used to draw the shape. No equivalent for this series of functions exists in the TRS-80 without modification. A shape approximated on the TRS-80 may be removed from the screen by POKing the addresses used previously in the DRAW approximation to Ø (see DRAW). |

### APPLE II PEEK, POKE, and CALL Statements and TRS-80 Approximations

| APPLE II | TRS-80 | Comments |
|----------|--------|----------|
| CALL −936 | CLS | Clears all characters and moves the cursor to the top left-most printing position |
| CALL −958 | PRINT CHR$(31) | Clears all characters from the current cursor position to the bottom of the screen |
| CALL −868 | PRINT CHR$(30) | Clears all characters to the right of the cursor |
| X=PEEK (−16384) | NONE | Reads keyboard for the value of X. If X>127, then the key has been pressed, and X will be the ASCII value of the key that was pressed |

|                        |                        | plus 128. Use:<br>A\$=INKEY\$:X=ASC(A\$)+128 |
|------------------------|------------------------|------------------------------------------------|
| POKE−16368,<br>Ø       | NONE                   | Resets keyboard strobe (not needed<br>in translation) |
| X=PEEK(36)             | X=POS(Ø)               | Returns a number indicating the<br>position of the cursor |

## APPLE II POKES Ignorable During a Translation into TRS-80

| | |
|---|---|
| POKE 22, x | Sets text window width |
| POKE 32, x | Sets left margin of display |
| POKE 33, x | Sets width of display |
| POKE 34, x | Sets top margin of display |
| POKE 35, x | Sets bottom margin of display |
| POKE 36, x | Moves cursor to horizontal position<br>x+1 from left of margin |
| POKE 37,x | Moves cursor to absolute vertical<br>position specified by x |
| POKE 50, 127 | Sets inverse mode in Integer BASIC |
| POKE 50, 255 | Sets normal mode in Integer BASIC |
| POKE−16303, Ø | Switches from color graphics to text<br>without resetting scrolling window |
| POKE−16304, Ø | Switches display mode to graphics<br>without clearing screen to black |
| POKE−16368, Ø | Resets keyboard strobe [after<br>PEEK(−16384)] |
| POKE−16302, Ø | Switches from mixed text and<br>graphics to full graphics |
| POKE−16301, Ø | Switches from full graphics to mixed<br>graphics and text |

### APPLE II POKES Ignorable During a Translation into TRS-80 (continued)

POKE $-16300$, $\emptyset$       Switches from page 2 to page 1

POKE $-16299$, $\emptyset$       Switches from page 1 to page 2

POKE $-16298$, $\emptyset$       Switches from HI-RES graphics to text

POKE $-16297$, $\emptyset$       Switches from text to same page of HI-RES graphics

POKE $-16296$, $\emptyset$ to POKE $-16289$, $\emptyset$       Commands dealing with GAME paddles

POKE 216, $\emptyset$       Resets error flag after error-handling routine

POKE $-16336$, $\emptyset$       Toggles speaker (Integer BASIC)

## 2.2 Conversion of PET into TRS-80

### Commands

| PET | TRS-80 | Comments |
|-----|--------|----------|
| ABS(x) | ABS(x) | Same function |
| AND | AND | Same function |
| ASC(string) | ASC(string) | Same function |
| CHR$(x) | CHR$(x) | Same function |
| CLOSE | NONE | Used to close logical file; not needed when inputting data from TRS-80 tapes |
| CLR | CLEAR | Same function |
| CMD | NONE | Similar to the TRS-80 IN command; reads IEEE port for input |
| CONT | CONT | Same function |
| COS(x) | COS(x) | Same function |
| DATA | DATA | Same function |
| DEF FN | NONE | Not available in Level II; each function will have to be calculated individually |
| DIM | DIM | Same function |
| END | END | Same function (usually optional) |
| EXP(x) | EXP(x) | Same function |
| FOR | FOR | Same function |
| FRE(x) | FRE(x) | Same function |
| GET# | NONE | Reads data tape; not needed with TRS-80 |

## Commands *(continued)*

| PET | TRS-80 | Comments |
|---|---|---|
| GET A | NONE | Reads keyboard for variable input; use A$=INKEY$:A=VAL(A$) |
| GET A$ | A$=INKEY$ | Same function |
| GOSUB n | GOSUB n | Same function |
| GOTO n | GOTO n | Same function |
| IF | IF | Same function |
| INPUT | INPUT | Same function |
| INPUT# | INPUT#− n | Same function (reads input from tape) |
| INT(x) | INT(x) | Same function |
| LEFT$ | LEFT$ | Same function |
| LEN(string) | LEN(string) | Same function |
| LET | LET | Same function |
| LIST | LIST | Same function |
| LOAD | LOAD | Same function |
| LOAD "file name" | LOAD "x" | Same function except that PET file names may contain 16 characters or more, and TRS-80 file labels can contain only one character. |
| MID$ | MID$ | Same function |
| NEW | NEW | Same function |
| NEXT | NEXT | Same function |
| ON x GOSUB | ON x GOSUB | Same function |
| ON x GOTO | ON x GOTO | Same function |
| OPEN | NONE | Opens logical file (similar to TRS-80 INPUT#); reads data from tape file. |
| OR | OR | Same function |

| | | |
|---|---|---|
| PEEK(addr) | PEEK(addr) | Same function except that the addresses will be different |
| POKE(addr) | POKE(addr) | Same function except that the addresses will be different |
| POS(x) | POS(x) | Same function |
| PRINT | PRINT | Same function |
| PRINT# | PRINT#− | Same function |
| READ | READ | Same function |
| REM | REM | Same function |
| RESTORE | RESTORE | Same function |
| RETURN | RETURN | Same function |
| RIGHT$ | RIGHT$ | Same function |
| RND(x) | RND(x) | Same function |
| RUN | RUN | Same function |
| SAVE | CSAVE"x" | Same function except that the TRS-80 needs a file label |
| SAVE"file name" | CSAVE"x" | Same function except that PET allows several characters and the TRS-80 allows only one |
| SGN(x) | SGN(x) | Same function |
| SIN(x) | SIN(x) | Same function |
| SPC(x) | STRING$ (x,32) | Same function with the extra use of the STRING$ function (32 is the ASCII code for space). The SPC(x) function places x spaces on the screen. |
| SQR(x) | SQR(x) | Same function |
| STOP | STOP | Same function |
| STR$ | STR$ | Same function |

**Commands** *(continued)*

| PET | TRS-80 | Comments |
|-----|--------|----------|
| SYS(addr) | SYSTEM | Similar function since the SYS function provides access to previously stored machine-language routines as does the SYSTEM command [USR(∅) may also be used] |
| TAB(x) | TAB(x) | Same function |
| TAN(x) | TAN(x) | Same function |
| THEN | THEN | Same function |
| TI$ | NONE | Returns time recorded on PET internal clock; sometimes used to time input for program functions |
| USR(x) | USR(∅) | Same function except that the TRS-80 will have only one USR available in Level II |
| VAL(string) | VAL(string) | Same function |
| VERIFY"file name" | CLOAD?"x" | Same function except that the TRS-80 allows only one character for a label |
| WAIT | NONE | Causes execution of a program to halt until a nonzero result of the argument in the WAIT statement is achieved |

## Other Indications

| PET/APPLE II | TRS-80 | Comments |
|---|---|---|
| % | % | Designated variables as INTEGERS |
| π | NONE | The value of PI must be inserted (3.1428) in programs using a variable |

## Pet Graphics

The PET has built-in graphics characters in ROM that are often printed on the screen by using PRINT CHR$(x), (x being the ASCII representation of the graphics character); these graphics characters are not available on the TRS-80. In order to compensate for them in a program, refer to Chart 4 in Appendix C, and replace the character with POKE graphics in the TRS-80.

## Cursor Control Characters

Each cursor control character is preceded by a PRINT command or used as a CHR$. The cursor control characters are listed in Section 3.2 (Chap. 3).

# Chapter 3

# CONVERSION OF TRS-80 AND PET PROGRAMS INTO APPLE II

This chapter is designed for easy conversion of TRS-80 and PET programs into APPLE II programs. The commands are listed in alphabetical order for quick reference. Several subroutines have been included so that you can approximate TRS-80 or PET commands that do not directly relate to AP-PLE II commands.

Graphics will be discussed from the standpoint of what can be done and what cannot be done, but for the most part, your imagination will be the best guide in trying to convert TRS-80 and PET graphics to APPLE II since APPLE II will allow you much more variety.

The format for this chapter is as follows:

*TRS-80/PET*      *APPLE II*
*Function*        *Function*          *Comments*

Every command with a direct relationship to APPLE II is included. Some APPLE II commands are not included, how-ever, since nothing in a TRS-80 or PET listing will relate to them (for example, CALL, POP, and the like). Subroutines and other conversion indicators that allow the APPLE II to per-form a TRS-80 or PET function are included in the comments section of each command.

Sample program conversions appear in Appendix B.

# 3.1 Conversion of TRS-80 into APPLE II

## Commands

| TRS-80 | APPLE II | Comments |
|--------|----------|----------|
| ABS(x) | ABS(x) | Same function |
| AND | AND | Same function |
| ASC(string) | ASC(string) | Same function |
| ATN(x) | ATN(x) | Same function |
| AUTO | AUTO | AUTO line numbering, available only in Integer BASIC |
| BREAK | CONTROL C | Same function |
| CDBL | None | Returns double-precision representation of a number |
| CHR$ | CHR$ | Same function |
| CINT | None | Returns integer of number |
| CLEAR | CLEAR | Same function |
| CLEAR nn | None | Reserves string space; not necessary in APPLE II |
| CLOAD | LOAD | Same function |
| CLOAD"X" | None | APPLE II does not load by label |
| CLOAD?"X" | None | Used to verify transfer of a program; not available in APPLE II |
| CLS | HOME | Same function |
| CONT | CONT | Same function |
| COS(x) | COS(x) | Same function |
| CSAVE | SAVE | Same function |
| CSAVE"X" | None | APPLE II does not save by label |
| CSNG | None | Returns a single-precision number |

## Commands *(continued)*

| TRS-80 | APPLE II | Comments |
|---|---|---|
| D | None | Defines variable as a double-precision number |
| DATA | DATA | Same function |
| DEFDBL | None | Defines a variable as double precision |
| DEFINT | None | Defines a variable as an integer (use % after a variable to approximate this function) |
| DEFSNG | None | Defines a variable as single precision |
| DELETE | DEL | Same function (deletes program lines) |
| DIM | DIM | Same function |
| E | E | Same function (scientific notation) |
| EDIT | None | EDIT mode not available in APPLE II |
| ELSE | None | ELSE is used in IF . . . THEN statements. Use separate IF . . . THEN statements when this command is encountered. For example: |
| | | 10 IFA=BTHENGOTO1000ELSE200 (TRS-80) |
| | | 10 IFA=BTHENGOTO1000 |
| | | 15 IFA<>BTHENGOTO200 |
| END | END | Same function |
| ERL | None | Returns line number of error; use X=PEEK(218)+PEEK(219)*256 to return line number of error |
| ERR/2+1 | PEEK(222) | Returns error code of error |
| EXP(x) | EXP(x) | Same function |
| FIX(x) | INT(x) | Same function |

| | | |
|---|---|---|
| FOR | FOR | Same function |
| FRE(string) | FRE(Ø) | Same function. Returns a negative number on a 48K machine; otherwise returns the amount of memory left available for programming |
| GOSUB | GOSUB | Same function |
| GOTO | GOTO | Same function |
| IF | IF | Same function |
| INKEY$ | GET(string) | Same function except that GET(string) stops program flow until key is pressed. INKEY$ does not wait for key input. If the very same function is desired, use the following: |
| | | X=PEEK(−16384);IF X>127 THEN GOTO xxxx |
| | | (If X>127, it means that a key was pressed) |
| INP(port) | IN# x | Inputs data from port [APPLE II is limited to Ø through 7 (Ø is keyboard)] |
| INPUT | INPUT | Same function |
| INPUT # | RECALL x | Same function when used with variables; use subroutine 3 in Appendix A for recalling strings |
| INT | INT | Same function |
| LEFT$ | LEFT$ | Same function |
| LEN(string) | LEN(string) | Same function |
| LET | LET | Same function |
| LIST | LIST | Same function |
| LLIST | None | Causes LIST to be output to printer; use PR#1 (if printer card is in slot 1) and then LIST |

| TRS-80 | APPLE II | Comments |
|---|---|---|
| LOG(x) | LOG(x) | Same function |
| LPRINT | None | Causes display to be output to printer; use PR#1 to transfer printing to printer |
| MEM | FRE(∅) | Returns amount of free memory |
| MID$ | MID$ | Same function |
| NEW | NEW | Same function |
| NEXT | NEXT | Same function |
| NOT | NOT | Same function |
| ON ERROR GOTO | ON ERR GOTO | Same function |
| ON . . GOSUB | ON . . GOSUB | Same function |
| ON . . GOTO | ON . . GOTO | Same function |
| OR | OR | Same function |
| OUT(port) | PR# x | Although PR# x is similar to OUT, all output is transferred to slot x, not just a specific byte as with OUT (x must be a number from ∅ to 7); if no device is connected, computer will "hang" |
| PEEK(addr) | PEEK(addr) | Same function, but addresses are different (see list of common PEEKs) |
| POINT(x,y) | None | No direct function relates to this command; its purpose is to check whether a point on the screen is "ON." It can be approximated by using the SCRN(x,y) function. The SCRN(x,y) function returns a color |

| | | |
|---|---|---|
| | | code of the spot on the screen to allow you to evaluate the color code and determine whether the graphics block is on. |
| POKE(addr,x) | POKE(addr,x) | Same function, but addresses are different |
| POS(x) | POS(x) | Same function |
| PRINT | PRINT | Same function |
| PRINT @ | None | Causes output to be placed on the screen at a specific point (see Chart 1 in Appendix C) |
| PRINT#−1 | STORE A | See Subroutine 2 in Appendix A |
| PRINT USING | None | See Subroutine 1 in Appendix A |
| RANDOM | None | Reseeds random numbers; not necessary with APPLE II |
| READ | READ | Same function |
| REM | REM | Same function |
| RESET(x,y) | PLOT(x,y) | To reset a block of graphics in both HI-RES and LO-RES, simply PLOT the same coordinates in the background color |
| RESTORE | RESTORE | Same function |
| RESUME | RESUME | Same function |
| RETURN | RETURN | Same function |
| RIGHT$ | RIGHT$ | Same function |
| RND(x) | RND(x) | RND(∅) is the same, but if the RND number is greater than 1, use Subroutine 5 in Appendix A |
| RUN | RUN | Same function |
| SET(x,y) | PLOT(x,y) | Same function except that field limits are: X=39, Y=47 (instead of |

## Commands *(continued)*

| TRS-80 | APPLE II | Comments |
|--------|----------|----------|
| | | X=127, Y=45). "GR" or "HGR" must be used before a PLOT. |
| SGN(x) | SGN(x) | Same function |
| SIN(x) | SIN(x) | Same function |
| SQR(x) | SQR(x) | Same function |
| STOP | STOP | Same function |
| STR$ | STR$ | Same function |
| STRING$ | None | See Subroutine 4 |
| SYSTEM | None | This command allows access to machine-language programs; use CALL-151 or press the RESET key |
| TAB | TAB | Same function |
| TAN(x) | TAN(x) | Same function |
| THEN | THEN | Same function |
| TROFF | NOTRACE | Same function |
| TRON | TRACE | Same function |
| USR(x) | USR(x) | Same function (address for the USR function on the TRS-80 is POKED into addresses 16526 and 16527). Only one USR(x) call is allowed in TRS-80 Level II. |
| VAL(string) | VAL(string) | Same function |
| VARPTR | None | Returns decimal location of a variable stored in memory |

## Special Characters and Abbreviations

| TRS-80 | APPLE II | Comments |
|--------|----------|----------|
| ENTER | RETURN | Same function |
| ← | ← | Backspace and delete last character |
| : | : | Same function (statement delimiter) |
| CLEAR | CLEAR | Resets all variables and strings to NULL; arrays have to be redimensioned after CLEAR |
| SHIFT@ | CONTROL S | Interrupts program or listing; pressing any key will cause program or listing to resume (CONTROL S is available only with the AUTOSTART ROM; other models use CONTROL C) |
| BREAK | CONTROL C | Stops program or listing and returns to BASIC; type CONT to continue |
| RESET | RESET | Causes program execution to cease and places computer in MONITOR mode (CONTROL C will return you to BASIC) |
| ? | ? | Same function (abbreviation for PRINT) |

## Type Declaration Characters

| Character | Type | Example |
|-----------|------|---------|
| $ | String | A$, AF$ |
| % | Integer | A%, AF% |
| E | Exponential | 1.23E+10 |

### Arithmetic Operators

+    Add           –    Subtract         *    Multiply
  /    Divide            ∧    Exponentiate (2∧3 = 8)

### String Operators

+    Concatenate (string together)

### Relational Operators

| Symbol | Meaning in Numerics | Meaning in Strings |
|---|---|---|
| < | Is less than | Precedes |
| > | Is greater than | Follows |
| = | Is equal to | Equals |
| <= or =< | Is less than or equal | Precedes or equals |
| >= or => | Is greater than or equal | Follows or equals |
| <> or >< | Does not equal | Does not equal |

### Order of Operation

∧        Exponentiation

*, /     Multiplication, division

+, –     Addition, subtraction

AND
OR

## 3.2 Translation of PET into APPLE II

### Commands

| PET | APPLE II | Comments |
|---|---|---|
| ABS(x) | ABS(x) | Same function |
| AND | AND | Same function |
| ASC(string) | ASC(string) | Same function |
| CHR$(x) | CHR$(x) | Same function |
| CLOSE | None | Used to close a logical file but not needed when reading data from APPLE II tapes |
| CLR | CLEAR | Same function |
| CMD | None | Similar to APPLE II IN#; reads IEEE port for input |
| CONT | CONT | Same function |
| COS(x) | COS(x) | Same function |
| DATA | DATA | Same function |
| DEF FN | DEF FN | Same function (string functions cannot be defined) |
| DIM | DIM | Same function |
| END | END | Same function (optional in APPLE II, mandatory in INTEGER) |
| EXP(X) | EXP(X) | Same function |
| FOR | FOR | Same function |
| FRE(x) | FRE(x) | Same function. Returns a negative number on a 48k machine; otherwise returns the amount of memory left available for programming |

**Commands** *(continued)*

| PET | APPLE II | Comments |
|---|---|---|
| GET# | None | Used to read a character from data tape, but not needed with APPLE II |
| GET A | GET A | Same function, but APPLE II recommends using the keyboard strobe [X=PEEK(–16384)] to avoid errors |
| GET A$ | GET A$ | Same function except that APPLE II program execution halts until a key is pressed and PET program execution continues unless a key is pressed. |
| GOSUB n | GOSUB n | Same function |
| GOTO n | GOTO n | Same function |
| IF | IF | Same function |
| INPUT | INPUT | Same function |
| INPUT# | RECALL n | Same function except that conversion of data stored as strings must be handled in accordance with Subroutine 3 in Appendix A |
| INT(x) | INT(x) | Same function |
| LEFT$ | LEFT$ | Same function |
| LEN(string) | LEN(string) | Same function |
| LET | LET | Same function (optional) |
| LIST | LIST | Same function |
| LOAD | LOAD | Same function (loads tape when file name is not present) |
| LOAD "file name" | None | APPLE II does not store programs by file name except on disk |

| | | |
|---|---|---|
| MID$ | MID$ | Same function |
| NEW | NEW | Same function |
| NEXT | NEXT | Same function |
| ON x GOSUB | ON x GOSUB | Same function |
| ON x GOTO | ON x GOTO | Same function |
| OPEN | None | Opens logical file, but not necessary in APPLE II |
| OR | OR | Same function |
| PEEK(addr) | PEEK(addr) | Same function, but addresses are different |
| POKE(addr) | POKE(addr) | Same function, but addresses are different |
| POS(x) | POS(x) | Same function |
| PRINT | PRINT | Same function |
| PRINT # | STORE A | Same function (stores data on tape). String storage must be handled in accordance with Subroutine 2 in Appendix A |
| READ | READ | Same function |
| REM | REM | Same function |
| RESTORE | RESTORE | Same function |
| RETURN | RETURN | Same function |
| RIGHT$ | RIGHT$ | Same function |
| RND(x) | RND(x) | Same function |
| RUN | RUN | Same function |
| SAVE | SAVE | Same function (saves files on tape when file name is not used) |
| SAVE "file name" | None | APPLE II does not save programs by file name except on disk |

### Commands *(continued)*

| PET | APPLE II | Comments |
|---|---|---|
| SGN(x) | SGN(x) | Same function |
| SIN(x) | SIN(x) | Same function |
| SPC(x) | SPC(x) | Same function |
| SQR(x) | SQR(x) | Same function |
| STOP | STOP | Same function (causes bell to sound in APPLE II) |
| STR$ | STR$ | Same function |
| SYS(addr) | CALL addr | Generally the same function, but addresses will differ. (This command branches from a BASIC program to a machine-language routine.) |
| TAB(x) | TAB(x) | Same function |
| TAN(x) | TAN(x) | Same function |
| THEN | THEN | Same function |
| TI$ | None | Returns time recorded on PET internal clock; sometimes used to time input for program functions |
| USR(x) | USR(x) | Same function (note that addresses are not the same) |
| VAL(string) | VAL(string) | Same function |
| VERIFY "file name" | None | Used to verify program dump on tape but not available or necessary on APPLE II |
| WAIT | WAIT | Same function, but since timing in the PET and APPLE II is different, make note of the approximate timing desired for the program and adjust accordingly |

## Other Indications

| PET | APPLE II | Comments |
|-----|----------|----------|
| % | % | Designates a variable as an integer |
| $\pi$ | PI=3.1428 | The value of pi must be substituted for the symbol $\pi$ |

## PET Graphics

The PET has a built-in character ROM for various graphic characters. In order to compensate for this feature, you must create your own graphic version of the symbols provided on the PET. Chart 4 in Appendix C gives the character set and the ASCII equivalents. If you encounter POKE graphics, refer to this character set to determine what is intended in the program.

## Cursor and Control Characters

Each cursor and control character is preceded by a PRINT command or is used as a CHR$. The cursor and control characters, their functions, and the corresponding ASCII characters and APPLE II commands are as follows:

| Character | Function | ASCII Value | APPLE II Command |
|---|---|---|---|
| ♡ | Clear screen and home cursor | 147 | HOME |
| ] | Cursor right | 29 | PRINT CHR$(9) |
| O | Cursor up | 145 | Not available |
| Q | Cursor down | 17 | Not available |
| S | Home cursor | 19 | CALL −936 or HOME |
| I | Cursor left | 157 | |
| R | Reverse field | 18 | INVERSE |
| — | Reset normal field | 146 | NORMAL |
| I | Insert character | 148 | Not used |
| T | Delete character | 20 | Not used |

# Chapter 4
# CONVERSION OF TRS-80 AND APPLE II PROGRAMS INTO PET

This chapter is designed for easy conversion of TRS-80 and APPLE II programs into PET. The commands are in alphabetical order for quick reference. Moreover, several subroutines are included in the comments column to allow you to approximate PET commands that do not directly relate to APPLE II commands.

Graphics will be discussed from the standpoint of what can be done and what cannot be done, but for the most part your imagination will be the best guide in trying to convert TRS-80 and APPLE II graphics to PET.

The format for this chapter is as follows:

*TRS-80/APPLE II*  　　　*PET Function*  　　　*Comments*
　　*Function*

Every command that has a direct relationship to PET is included. Some PET commands have been omitted if they do not relate to the functions of either the TRS-80 or APPLE II. Subroutines and other conversion indicators that allow the PET to perform a TRS-80 or APPLE II function are mentioned in the comments section at the side of each command.

## 4.1 Conversion of TRS-80 into PET

This section is designed for easy conversion of TRS-80 programs into PET. In general, the commands are in the order they are found in the TRS-80 Level II manual. Several subroutines are included to allow you to approximate TRS-80 commands that do not directly relate to PET commands.

Graphics will be discussed from the standpoint of what can be done and what can't be done, but, for the most part, your own imagination will serve you best in trying to convert the TRS-80 graphics.

The format for this guide is as follows:

*TRS-80 Function     PET Function     Comments*

Each TRS-80 command that has a direct relationship to PET is included. Subroutines and other conversion indicators that allow the PET to perform a TRS-80 function are listed in the comments section at the side of each command.

Sample programs with conversions are included in Appendix B.

Since timing loops work faster for the PET by a factor of about two, you will need to change a statement such as FOR X=1 TO 1000:NEXT, for example, to FOR X=1 to 2000 NEXT to maintain approximately the same timing.

## Commands

| TRS-80 | PET | Comments |
|--------|-----|----------|
| AUTO | None | |
| CLEAR | CLR | Sets numeric variables to zero, strings to NULL, and arrays to zero; arrays must be redimensioned. |
| CLEAR n | None | PET reserves space for strings by itself |
| CONT | CONT | Continue after STOP |
| DELETE mm-nn | None | Deletes line mm to nn |
| EDIT | None | |
| LIST mm-nn | LIST mm-nn | LIST linenum to linenum |

| | | |
|---|---|---|
| LIST nn | LIST nn | LIST linenum |
| LIST nn- | LIST nn- | LIST from linenum to end of program |
| LIST | LIST | LIST entire program |
| NEW | NEW | Deletes entire program and resets all variables |
| RUN | RUN | Executes program from beginning |
| RUNnn | RUNnn | RUN program from line nn |
| TRON | None | Turns on TRACE mode |
| TROFF | None | Turns off TRACE mode |
| SYSTEM | SYS | Used to load machine-language programs (use MONITOR commands) |
| CLOAD | LOAD | Loads programs from cassette |
| CLOAD "name" | LOAD "name" | LOAD (name) program |
| CLOAD? "name" | VERIFY "name" | VERIFY (name) program |
| CSAVE | SAVE | SAVE program on cassette |
| CSAVE "name" | SAVE "name" | SAVE (name) program |

## Input/Output

| TRS-80 | PET | Comments |
|---|---|---|
| PRINT | PRINT | Same function |
| PRINT @ | None | See Chart 1 in Appendix C |
| PRINT TAB (n) | PRINT TAB (n) | Same function except that the maximum TAB field is 39 instead of 63 |
| PRINT USING | None | See Subroutine 1 in Appendix A |
| INPUT | INPUT | Same function |
| DATA | DATA | Same function |
| READ | READ | Same function |
| RESTORE | RESTORE | Same function |
| PRINT #-1 | PRINT # 1 | Prints data on tape |
| INPUT #-1 | INPUT # 1 | Recalls data previously stored on tape |

## Program Statements

| TRS-80 | PET | Comments |
|---|---|---|
| DEFINT | None | Each variable to be used as an integer must be labeled with the % sign (that is, a%, c%) |
| DEFSNG | None | Designates a number as single-precision |
| DEFDBL | None | Designates a number as double-precision |
| DEFSTR | None | Defines variable to be treated as a string variable |
| DIM | DIM | Same function, but variables may be used for DIM statements rather than constants: for example, 10   INPUT |

|  |  | "HOW MANY DIMENSIONS"; X and 20   DIM A(X), B(X) |
| --- | --- | --- |
| LET | LET | Same function (optional) |
| END | END | Same function |
| STOP | STOP | Same function; STOPs execution in program and prints BREAK IN linenum |
| GOTO nn | GOTO nn | Causes program to branch to linenum nn; can also be used in the IMMEDIATE mode to cause the program to begin at a specified point without resetting all variables (used instead of RUN) |
| GOSUB nn | GOSUB nn | Same function |
| RETURN | RETURN | Same function |
| On n GOTO nn | ON n GOTO nn | Same function |
| ON n GOSUB nn | Same function |  |
| FOR name =expTOexpSTEPn Same function |  |  |
| NEXT name | NEXT name | Same function (name is optional) |
| ERROR code | None |  |
| On ERROR GOTO | None |  |
| RESUME | None |  |
| REM | REM | Same function |
| IF true/false | IFtrue/false | Same function |
| THEN | THEN | Same function (optional in most situations) |
| ELSE | None | Another "IF" statement must be used in PET |

### String Input/Output

| TRS-80 | PET | Comments |
|--------|-----|----------|
| ASC (string) | ASC (string) | Same function |
| CHR$(exp) | CHR$(exp) | Same function |
| FRE(string) | FRE(exp) | Same function [FRE(exp) performs housecleaning; see PET manual] |
| INKEY$ | GETexp$ | Same function |
| LEFT$(string,n) | LEFT$(string,n) | Same function |
| LEN(string) | LEN(string) | Same function |
| MID$(string,p,n) | MID$(string,p,n) | Same function |
| RIGHT$(string,n) | RIGHT$(string,n) | Same function |
| STR$(exp) | STR$(exp) | Same function |
| STRING$ (n,char or number) | None | See Subroutine 4 in Appendix A |
| VAL(string) | | Same function |

### Arithmetic Functions

| TRS-80 | PET | Comments |
|--------|-----|----------|
| ABS(x) | ABS(x) | Same function |
| ATN(x) | ATN(x) | Same function |
| CDBL(x) | None | |
| CINT(x) | None | |
| COS(x) | COS(x) | Same function |
| CSNG(x) | None | |
| EXP(x) | EXP(x) | Same function |

| FIX(x) | INT(x) | Same function except that if x is negative, FIX(x)=INT(x)+1 |
|--------|--------|--------------------------------------------------------------|
| INT(x) | INT(x) | Same function |
| LOG(x) | LOG(x) | Same function |
| RANDOM | None | |
| RND(∅) | RND(∅) | Same function |
| RND(x) | None | See Subroutine 5 in Appendix A |
| SGN(x) | SGN(x) | Same function |
| SIN(x) | SIN(x) | Same function |
| TAN(x) | TAN(x) | Same function |

## Special Features

| TRS-80 | PET | Comments |
|--------|-----|----------|
| SET(x,y) | None | |
| RESET(x,y) | None | |
| CLS | PRINT "🖤" | Clears screen and homes cursor |
| POINT(x,y) | None | |
| ERL | None | |
| ERR/2+1 | None | |
| INP(port) | INPUT # | IN# x is limited to numbers from ∅ to 3∅ (∅ is keyboard |
| MEM | FRE(∅) | Same function |
| OUT port, value | PR# x | PR# x is similar to OUT except that *all* output is transferred to slot x, not just a specific byte (x must be a number from ∅ to 3∅). PR# ∅ is output to screen. If no device is connected to the specified slot, the computer will "hang." |

### Special Features (continued)

| | | |
|---|---|---|
| PEEK(addr) | PEEK(addr) | Same function, but the addresses are different |
| POKE(addr) | POKE(addr) | Same function, but the addresses are different |
| POS(x) | POS(x) | Same function; returns the current position of the cursor (number within the parentheses is a dummy number) |
| USR(x) | USR(x) | Same function |
| VARPTR (variable name) | None | Returns location in memory where (variable name) is stored |

### Special Characters and Abbreviations

| TRS-80 | PET | Comments |
|---|---|---|
| ENTER | RETURN | Same function |
| ← | INST DEL | Backspaces and deletes last character Same function (statement delimiter) |
| CLEAR | CLR | Resets all variables and strings to NULL; arrays have to be redimensioned after CLEAR |
| SHIFT@ | RUN STOP | Stops program execution, but requires CONT to continue |
| BREAK | RUN STOP | Stops program execution, but requires CONT to continue |
| RESET | None | |
| ? | ? | Abbreviation for PRINT |

## Type Declaration Characters

| Character | Type | Examples |
|-----------|------|----------|
| $ | String | A$, AF$ |
| % | Integer | A%, AF% |
| E | Exponential | 1.23E+Ø |

## Arithmetic Operators

| + | Add | − | Subtract | * Multiply |
|---|-----|---|----------|------------|
| / | Divide | ↑ | Exponentiate | (2 ↑ 3 = 8) |

## String Operators

+ Concatenate (string together)

## Relational Operators

| Symbol | Meaning in Numerics | Meaning in Strings |
|--------|---------------------|--------------------|
| > | Is less than | Precedes |
| < | Is greater than | Follows |
| = | Is equal to | Equals |
| >= or => | Is less than or equal | Precedes or equals |
| <= or =< | Is greater than or equal | Follows or equals |
| <> or >< | Does not equal | Does not equal |

| | |
|---|---|
| ( ) | Parentheses |
| ↑ | Exponentiation |
| *,/ | Multiplication, division |
| +, − | Addition, subtraction |

AND

OR

# 4.2 Conversion of APPLE II into PET

This section is designed for easy conversion of APPLE II programs into PET. In general, the commands are in the order they are found in the APPLE II manual. Several subroutines are included in the comments column to allow you to approximate PET commands that do not directly relate to APPLE II commands.

Graphics will be discussed from the standpoint of what can be done and what can't be done, but for the most part your imagination will serve you best in trying to convert the PET graphics, since APPLE II graphics allow much more variety.

The format for this guide is as follows:

*APPLE II Function*    *PET Function*    *Comments*

Each APPLE II command that has a direct relationship to PET is included. Subroutines and other conversion indicators to allow the PET to perform an APPLE II function are listed in the comments section at the side of each command.

Sample programs with conversions are included in Appendix B.

Timing loops work faster for the APPLE II by a factor of about two. You will need to change a statement such as FOR X=1 TO 2000:NEXT, for example, to FOR X=1 TO 1000:NEXT to maintain approximately the same timing.

## Commands

| APPLE II | PET | Comments |
|---|---|---|
| ABS(x) | ABS(x) | Same function |
| Arrow keys | None | Use cursor control keys |
| ASC(string) | ASC(string) | Same function |
| ATN | ATN | Same function |
| CALL | None | See common calls at end of section |
| CHR$(x) | CHR$(x) | Same function |
| CLEAR | CLR | Clears all variables, arrays, and strings to zero |
| COLOR | None | No color is available on PET |
| CONT | CONT | Same function |
| COS | COS | Same function |
| ctrl C | RUN STOP | Stops program execution but requires CONT to continue |
| ctrl X | None | Not available in PET |
| DATA | DATA | Same function |
| DEF FN(x) | DEF FN(x) | Same function (string functions cannot be defined) |
| DEL | None | Deletes lines from program |
| DIM | DIM | Same function |
| DRAW | None | Not necessary in PET |
| END | END | Same function |
| EXP | EXP | Same function |
| FLASH | None | Blinks words on screen; not applicable in PET |

**Commands** *(continued)*

| *APPLE II* | *PET* | *Comments* |
|---|---|---|
| FOR. . . TO. . . STEP | FOR. . . TO. . . STEP | Same function |
| FRE(x) | FRE(x) | Same function |
| GET | GET | Same function |
| GOSUB | GOSUB | Same function |
| GOTO | GOTO | Same function |
| GR | None | Sets graphics mode in APPLE II; not necessary in PET |
| HCOLOR | None | Sets color in APPLE II graphics; not necessary in PET |
| HGR | None | Sets high-resolution graphics mode; not necessary in PET |
| HGR2 | None | Sets high-resolution graphics; not necessary in PET |
| HIMEM: | None | Sets a point in memory above which machine operation will not interfere; not necessary in PET |
| HLIN | None | Draws a horizontal line between points x and y; not available in PET |
| HOME | Print "♥" | Same function |
| HPLOT | None | Plots a point (x,y) on screen. Use POKE x (32768 to 33792) |
| HTABx | None | Sets horizontal position of cursor on a specific line; not available in PET |
| IF. . . GOTO | IF. . . GOTO | Same function |

| | | |
|---|---|---|
| IF. . . THEN | IF. . . THEN | Same function |
| INPUT | INPUT | Same function |
| INT(x) | INT(x) | Same function |
| INVERSE | PRINT " R " | Same function |
| IN# | INPUT# | Reads DATA from I/O device; device numbers will differ |
| LEFT$ | LEFT$ | Same function |
| ← | SHIFT CRSR | Backspace over last character |
| LEN | LEN | Same function |
| LET | LET | Same function (optional) |
| LIST | LIST | Same function |
| LIST x-y | LIST x-y | Same function |
| LOAD | LOAD | Same function |
| LOG | LOG | Same function |
| LOMEM | None | Sets a point in memory below which machine operation will not interfere; not necessary in PET |
| MID$ | MID$ | Same function |
| NEW | NEW | Same function |
| NEXT | NEXT | Same function |
| NORMAL | PRINT " ▮ " | Same function |
| NOTRACE | None | Turns trace off; not available in PET |
| ON. . . GOSUB | ON. . GOSUB | Same function |
| ON. . . GOTO | ON. . . GOTO | Same function |
| ONERR GOTO | None | On encountering an error program, branches to specific line; not available in PET |

| APPLE II | PET | Comments |
|---|---|---|
| PDL | None | Reads paddle functions on APPLE II; not available in PET |
| PEEK(x) | PEEK(x) | Same function, but addresses will differ |
| PLOT | None | See HPLOT |
| POKE(addr,x) | POKE(addr,x) | Same function, but POKE addresses will differ |
| POP | None | Retrieves return addresses from "stack" of returns; not necessary in PET |
| POS(X) | POS(X) | Same function |
| PRINT | PRINT | Same function |
| PR# | PRINT# | Writes data to I/O device; device numbers will differ |
| READ | READ | Same function |
| RECALL | GET# or INPUT# | Same function |
| REM | REM | Same function |
| REPEAT | None | |
| REPEAT | None | |
| RESTORE | RESTORE | Same function |
| RESUME | None | After "ONERR GOTO," program function continues; not available in PET |
| RETURN | RETURN | Same function |
| RIGHT$ | RIGHT$ | Same function |
| → | ⬛CRSR | Same function |

| | | |
|---|---|---|
| ROT | None | Rotates a shape on machine; not available in PET |
| RND | RND | Same function |
| RUN | RUN | Same function |
| SAVE | SAVE | Same function |
| SCALE | None | Sets size of shape on screen |
| SCRN (x,y) | None | Returns color code of coordinates x,y; used to test point on screen; correlates to PEEK (ADDR) in PET |
| SGN | SGN | Same function |
| SHLOAD | None | Loads shape from tape stored data; not available in PET |
| SIN | SIN | Same function |
| SPC | SPC | Same function |
| SPEED | None | Adjust rate at which characters are displayed on the screen; not available in PET |
| SQR | SQR | Same function |
| STEP | STEP | Same function |
| STOP | STOP | Same function |
| STORE | PRINT # | Same function |
| STR$ | STR$ | Same function |
| TAB | TAB | Same function |
| TAN | TAN | Same function |
| TEXT | None | Returns program to text mode and turns off graphics; not necessary in PET |
| TRACE | None | Turns trace on |
| USR(X) | USR(X) | Same function |

## Commands *(continued)*

| APPLE II | PET | Comments |
|---|---|---|
| VAL(string) | VAL(string) | Same function |
| VLIN | None | Draws vertical line; not available in PET |
| VTAB(X) | None | Moves cursor X vertical spaces (uses cursor down characters with PET) |
| WAIT | WAIT | Same function |
| XDRAW | None | Erases shapes previously designed by a draw command or changes colors of a shape; not available in PET |

## Common APPLE II CALLS or POKES and PET Functions

| APPLE II | Comments |
|---|---|
| PEEK (addr) | Same function as PEEK (addr) in PET, but the addresses are different |
| POKE (addr) | Same function as POKE (addr) in PET, but the addresses are different |
| POKE 32,X)<br>POKE 33,X)<br>POKE 34,X)<br>POKE 35,X) | These four commands relate to setting text window; not necessary in PET |
| POKE −16289 through<br>POKE −16296 | Commands dealing with game control; not necessary in PET |
| POKE −16297 through<br>POKE −16304 | Commands related to graphics and text screens; not necessary in PET |
| POKE −16368,0 | Resets keyboard stroke; not necessary in PET |
| X = PEEK (−16384) | Reads keyboard; PET uses GET A for this function |
| CALL −936 | Clears all characters on screen; same as PRINT " ■ " on PET |

# Appendix A:
# SUBROUTINES

## SUBROUTINE No. 1
## (PRINT USING Function)

The PRINT USING command is used to format output in a specific manner. The following subroutine allows you to indicate what output you want.

```
5000  A$=STR$(N):FORX=1TOLEN(A$)
5010  IFMID$(A$,X,1)=".'"THENGOTO5040
5020  NEXTX:AA$=A$
5030  RETURN
5040  A$=A$+"000000000000":AA$=LEFT$(A$,X+Z)
5050  RETURN
```

*Sample Program*

```
10   PRINT:INPUT"INPUT NUMBER OF DECIMAL PLACES";Z
20   INPUT"ENTER NUMBER TO BE FORMATTED";N
30   GOSUB5000
40   PRINT AA$
50   GOTO10
```

The program must have a predetermined value for the number of decimal places, Z, before the subroutine is entered.

## SUBROUTINE No. 2
## (STRING STORAGE)

To save strings, you must first convert them to variables. The following subroutine will do this for you:

```
10   DIM R(258)
20   R(Ø) = N :REM ** N IS THE NUMBER OF STRINGS TO BE
     STORED
```

```
30  FOR X =1 TO N
40  R(1) = X
50  R(2) = LEN(A$(X)) :REM ** A$ IS STRING TO BE SAVED
60  FOR Y = 3 TO LEN(A$(X))+2
70  R(Y) = ASC(MID$(A$(X),Y-2,1))
80  NEXT : STORE R : NEXT
```

Make sure that you DIMension an array large enough to accommodate the string being saved (in the program above, the array is set to 258, which is the maximum string size allowed).

## SUBROUTINE No. 3
## (STRING RECALL AND CONVERT)

To recall strings that have been previously stored as variables, use the following subroutine:

```
 90  PRINT"PRESS RETURN TO RECALL DATA ":GETZS
100  DIM S(260)
110  RECALL S
120  FOR Y = 3 TO S(2)+2
130  Y$ = CHR$(S(Y)):A$(1)=A$(1)+Y$
140  NEXT
150  FOR X = 2 TO S(0)
160  RECALL S
170  FOR Y = 3 TO S(2)+2
180  Y$ = CHR$(S(Y)):A$(X)=A$(X)+Y$
190  NEXT : NEXT
```

Make sure that you DIMension an array to carry A$(x).

## SUBROUTINE No. 4
## (STRING$ Function)

The STRING$ function allows you to print a number of characters or symbols in a row [that is, STRING$("*",30) returns a string of 30 asterisks]. To simulate this function, use the following:

```
10   INPUT X$ : REM *** X$=CHARACTER OR SYMBOL TO BE
     PRINTED
20   INPUT X : REM *** X =NUMBER OF TIMES TO REPEAT THE
     CHARACTER
30   FOR Y = 1 TO X
40   PRINT X$;
50   NEXT Y
```

or:

```
10   X$= "*" :X=30:FORTY=1TOX:PRINTX$;:NEXT
```

This program line exactly simulates the STRING$ function.

## SUBROUTINE No. 5
## (RANDOM Function)

The RND(∅) function returns a number from .000000 to .999999 in both languages. The RND(x) function in the TRS-80, however, returns a random number from 0 to x. To simulate this function in APPLESOFT II, use the following:

```
10000   Y = INT(RND(1)*X+.5)
```

where:

X = random number limit
Y = random number

# Appendix B:
# SAMPLE PROGRAM CONVERSION

| TRS-80 Program | APPLE II Conversion |
|---|---|
| 10 CLS-PRINT@Ø," "; | 10 HOME:HTAB1:VTAB1: PRINT" "; |
| 20 PRINT"TRS-80 SAMPLE" | 20 PRINT"APPLE II SAMPLE" |
| 30 A$="CENTER" | 30 A$="CENTER" |
| 40 X=544−LEN(A$)/2 | 40 X=20−(LEN(A$)/2) |
| 50 PRINT@X,A$ | 50 VTAB12:HTABX:PRINTA$ |
| 52 FORL=1TO800:NEXT | 52 FORL=1TO2400:NEXT |
| | 55 GR:COLOR=1 |
| 60 FORX=1TO127 | 60 FORX=ØTO39 |
| 70 Y=25 | 70 Y=12 |
| 80 SET(X,Y) | 80 PLOT X,Y |
| 90 NEXT | 90 NEXT |
| 100 FORX=1TO1000:NEXT | 100 FORX=1TO3000:NEXT |
| 110 PRINT"PRESS ENTER TO CONT" | 110 PRINT"PRESS RETURN TO CONT" |
| 120 X$=INKEY$:IFX$=" " GOTO120 | 120 GETX$:IFX$=" " GOTO120 |
| 130 GOTO10 | 130 TEXT:GOTO10 |

| TRS-80 Program | APPLE II Conversion |
|---|---|
| 10 CLS | 10 HOME:GR:COLOR=1 |
| 20 FORX=1TO127 | 20 FORX=ØTO39 |
| 30 Y=25 | 30 Y=12 |
| 40 SET(X,Y):NEXT | 40 PLOT X,Y:NEXT |
| 50 FOR L=1TO1000:NEXT | 50 FOR L=1TO3000:NEXT |
| 60 FOR X=1TO127 | 60 FOR X=ØTO39 |
| 70 RESET(X,Y):NEXT | 70 COLOR=Ø:PLOT X,Y:NEXT |
| 80 GOTO 80 | 80 GOTO 80 |

| APPLE II Program | | PET Conversion | |
|---|---|---|---|
| 10 | HOME: HTAB 1:VTAB 1:PRINT" "; | 10 | ?" ◻ ":PRINT""; |
| 20 | PRINT "APPLESOFT II SAMPLE" | 20 | PRINT"PET SAMPLE" |
| 30 | A$="CENTER" | 30 | A$="CENTER" |
| 40 | X=20−(LEN(A$)/2) | 40 | X=20−(LEN(A$)/2) |
| 50 | VTAB 6:HTABX:PRINT A$ | 50 | ?" QQQQQQ "; TAB(x);A$ |
| 52 | FORL=2TO1400:NEXT | 52 | FORL=1TO1600:NEXT |
| 60 | FORX=ØTO39 | 60 | FORX=ØTO39 |
| 65 | ?TAB(x);"*";:NEXT | 65 | ?TAB(x);"*";:NEXT |
| 70 | FORX=1TO1000 | 70 | FORX=1TO2000 |
| 80 | PRINT"PRESS RETURN TO CONT" | 80 | PRINT"PRESS RETURN TO CONT" |
| 90 | GETX$:IFX$=" "GOTO90 | 90 | GETX$:IFX$=" "GOTO90 |
| 100 | GOTO10 | 100 | GOTO10 |

| TRS-80 Program | | PET Conversion | |
|---|---|---|---|
| 10 | CLS:PRINT@Ø," "; | 10 | ?" ◻ ":PRINT" "; |
| 20 | PRINT"TRS-80SAMPLE" | 20 | PRINT"PET SAMPLE" |
| 30 | A$="CENTER" | 30 | A$="CENTER" |
| 40 | X=544−(LEN(A$)/2) | 40 | X=20−(LEN(A$)/2) |
| 50 | PRINT @X,A$ | 50 | ?" QQQQQQ QQQQQQ "; TAB(X);A$ |
| 60 | FORX=1TO63 | 60 | FORX=ØTO39 |
| 65 | ?TAB(x);"*";:NEXT | 65 | ?TAB(X);"*";:NEXT |
| 70 | FORX=1TO1000:NEXT | 70 | FORX=1TO2000:NEXT |
| 80 | PRINT"PRESS ENTER TO CONT" | 80 | PRINT"PRESS RETURN TO CONT" |
| 90 | X$=INKEY$:IFX$=" " GOTO90 | 90 | GET X$:IFX$=" "GOTO90 |
| 100 | GOTO10 | 100 | GOTO10 |

# Appendix C:
# CHARTS

## CHART 1

### Screen Coordinate Conversion from TRS-80 to APPLE II

| Left Margin | | | Center of Screen | | |
|---|---|---|---|---|---|
| PRINT@ | HTAB | VTAB | PRINT@ | HTAB | VTAB |
| Ø | 1 | 1 | 32 | 20 | 1 |
| 64 | 1 | 2 | 96 | 20 | 2 |
| 128 | 1 | 3 | 160 | 20 | 3 |
| 192 | 1 | 4 | 224 | 20 | 4 |
| 256 | 1 | 5 | 288 | 20 | 5 |
| 320 | 1 | 6 | 352 | 20 | 6 |
| 384 | 1 | 7 | 416 | 20 | 7 |
| 448 | 1 | 8 | 480 | 20 | 8 |
| 512 | 1 | 9 | 544 | 20 | 9 |
| 576 | 1 | 10 | 608 | 20 | 10 |
| 640 | 1 | 11 | 672 | 20 | 11 |
| 704 | 1 | 12 | 736 | 20 | 12 |
| 768 | 1 | 13 | 800 | 20 | 13 |
| 832 | 1 | 14 | 864 | 20 | 14 |
| 896 | 1 | 15 | 928 | 20 | 15 |
| 960 | 1 | 16 | 992 | 20 | 16 |
| 1024 | (Beyond screen limits) | | | | |

PRINT@ 544            HTAB20:VTAB12

HTAB and VTAB function with variables for numbers; for example:

```
10   VTAB 0:X=LEN(A$)/2:Y=20-X
20   HTAB Y
30   PRINT A$
```

The APPLE II has fewer characters allowed (40) on each line, but has nine extra vertical lines to accommodate printing (VTAB 1—25).

# CHART 2

## Screen Coordinate Conversion from TRS-80 to PET

| | Left Margin | | | Center of screen | |
|---|---|---|---|---|---|
| | | No. CURSORS | | | No. CURSORS |
| PRINT@: | TAB( ); | DOWN | PRINT@: | TAB( ); | DOWN |
| 0 | 1 | 1 | 32 | 20 | 1 |
| 64 | 1 | 2 | 96 | 20 | 2 |
| 128 | 1 | 3 | 160 | 20 | 3 |
| 192 | 1 | 4 | 224 | 20 | 4 |
| 256 | 1 | 5 | 288 | 20 | 5 |
| 320 | 1 | 6 | 352 | 20 | 6 |
| 384 | 1 | 7 | 416 | 20 | 7 |
| 448 | 1 | 8 | 480 | 20 | 8 |
| 512 | 1 | 9 | 544 | 20 | 9 |
| 576 | 1 | 10 | 608 | 20 | 10 |
| 640 | 1 | 11 | 672 | 20 | 11 |
| 704 | 1 | 12 | 736 | 20 | 12 |
| 768 | 1 | 13 | 800 | 20 | 13 |
| 832 | 1 | 14 | 864 | 20 | 14 |
| 896 | 1 | 15 | 928 | 20 | 15 |
| 960 | 1 | 16 | 992 | 20 | 16 |
| 1024 | (Beyond screen limits) | | | | |

TAB functions with variables for numbers; for example:

```
10  A$="HELLO"
20  PRINT "S": X=LEN(A$)/2:Y=20−X
30  PRINT TAB (Y);
40  PRINT A$
```

The PET has less characters allowed (40) on each line, but you have nine extra vertical lines to accommodate printing.

CHART 3

# Screen Coordinate Conversion from APPLE II to PET

| Left Margin | | | | Center of Screen | | | |
|:---:|:---:|:---:|:---:|:---:|:---:|:---:|:---:|
| | | | No. CURSORS | | | | No. CURSORS |
| HTAB | VTAB | TAB( ); | DOWN | HTAB | VTAB | TAB( ); | DOWN |
| 1 | 1 | 1 | 1 | 20 | 1 | 20 | 1 |
| 1 | 2 | 1 | 2 | 20 | 2 | 20 | 2 |
| 1 | 3 | 1 | 3 | 20 | 3 | 20 | 3 |
| 1 | 4 | 1 | 4 | 20 | 4 | 20 | 4 |
| 1 | 5 | 1 | 5 | 20 | 5 | 20 | 5 |
| 1 | 6 | 1 | 6 | 20 | 6 | 20 | 6 |
| 1 | 7 | 1 | 7 | 20 | 7 | 20 | 7 |
| 1 | 8 | 1 | 8 | 20 | 8 | 20 | 8 |
| 1 | 9 | 1 | 9 | 20 | 9 | 20 | 9 |
| 1 | 10 | 1 | 10 | 20 | 10 | 20 | 10 |
| 1 | 11 | 1 | 11 | 20 | 11 | 20 | 11 |
| 1 | 12 | 1 | 12 | 20 | 12 | 20 | 12 |
| 1 | 13 | 1 | 13 | 20 | 13 | 20 | 13 |
| 1 | 14 | 1 | 14 | 20 | 14 | 20 | 14 |
| 1 | 15 | 1 | 15 | 20 | 15 | 20 | 15 |
| 1 | 16 | 1 | 16 | 20 | 16 | 20 | 16 |

TAB functions with variables for numbers; for example:

```
10  A$="HELLO"
20  PRINT "S": X=LEN(A$)/2:Y=20-X
30  PRINT TAB (Y);
40  PRINT A$
```

CHART 4

## Pet Graphic Set

| B  6 | 0 | 0 | 0 | 0 | 1 | 1 | 1 | 1 |
| I  5 | 0 | 0 | 1 | 1 | 0 | 0 | 1 | 1 |
| T  4 | 0 | 1 | 0 | 1 | 0 | 1 | 0 | 1 |
| 3210 | | | | | | | | |
| --- | --- | --- | --- | --- | --- | --- | --- | --- |
| 0000 | @ | P |   | 0 | — | ⌐ |   | ⌐ |
| 0001 | A | Q | ! | 1 | ♠ | ● | ▮ | ⊥ |
| 0010 | B | R | .. | 2 | ▮ | — | ▬ | ⊤ |
| 0011 | C | S | # | 3 | — | ♥ |   | ⊣ |
| 0100 | D | T | $ | 4 | | | ─ | │ |
| 0101 | E | U | % | 5 | | ╱ | │ | ▐ |
| 0110 | F | V | & | 6 | — | ✕ | ▓ | ▌ |
| 0111 | G | W | ′ | 7 | │ | ○ | │ | ─ |
| 1000 | H | X | ( | 8 | │ | ♣ | ▒ | ▀ |
| 1001 | I | Y | ) | 9 | ╲ | │ | ▜ | ▄ |
| 1010 | J | Z | ∗ | : | ╲ | ♦ | │ | ⌐ |
| 1011 | K | [ | + | ; | ╱ | + | ├ | ■ |
| 1100 | L | \ | , | < | └ | ▒ | ■ | ■ |
| 1101 | M | ] | − | = | ╲ | │ | ⌐ | ┘ |
| 1110 | N | ↑ | . | > | ╱ | π | ┐ | ■ |
| 1111 | O | ← | / | ? | ┌ | ◣ | ─ | ◥ |

| Character | Screen Memory Location | Character | Screen Memory Location |
|---|---|---|---|
| @ | 0000000 | \ | 1100001 |
| A | 0000001 | ] | 1101001 |
| B | 0000010 | ↑ | 1110001 |
| C | 0000011 | ← | 1111001 |
| D | 0000100 |  | 0000010 |
| E | 0000101 | ! | 0001010 |
| F | 0000110 | .. | 0010010 |
| G | 0000111 | # | 0011010 |
| H | 0001000 | $ | 0100010 |
| I | 0001001 | % | 0101010 |
| J | 0001010 | & | 0110010 |
| K | 0001011 | ' | 0111010 |
| L | 0001100 | ( | 1000010 |
| M | 0001101 | ) | 1001010 |
| N | 0001110 | * | 1010010 |
| O | 0001111 | + | 1011010 |
| P | 0001000 | , | 1100010 |
| Q | 0001001 | − | 1101010 |
| R | 0010001 | . | 1110010 |
| S | 0011001 | / | 1111010 |
| T | 0100001 | 0 | 0000011 |
| U | 0101001 | 1 | 0001011 |
| V | 0110001 | 2 | 0010011 |
| W | 0111001 | 3 | 0011011 |
| X | 1000001 | 4 | 0100011 |
| Y | 1001001 | 5 | 0101011 |
| Z | 1010001 | 6 | 0110011 |
| [ | 1011001 | 7 | 0111011 |

| Character | Screen Memory Location | Character | Screen Memory Location |
|---|---|---|---|
| 8 | 1000011 | \| | 0100101 |
| 9 | 1001011 | ⁄ | 0101101 |
| : | 1010011 | × | 0110101 |
| ; | 1011011 | ○ | 0111101 |
| < | 1100011 | ♠ | 1000101 |
| = | 1101011 | \| | 1001101 |
| > | 1110011 | ♦ | 1010101 |
| ? | 1111011 | + | 1011101 |
| — | 0000100 | ▒ | 1100101 |
| ♠ | 0001100 | \| | 1101101 |
| \| | 0010100 | π | 1110101 |
| — | 0011100 | ◥ | 1111101 |
|  | 0100100 |  | 0000110 |
|  | 0101100 | ▮ | 0001110 |
| — | 0110100 | ▬ | 0010110 |
| \| | 0111100 |  | 0011110 |
| \| | 1000100 | — | 0100110 |
| ↖ | 1001100 | \| | 0101110 |
| ↘ | 1010100 | ▓ | 0110110 |
| ↗ | 1011100 | \| | 0111110 |
| L | 1100100 | ▒ | 1000110 |
| ＼ | 1101100 | ◣ | 1001110 |
| ／ | 1110100 | \| | 1010110 |
| Γ | 1111100 | ⊢ | 1011110 |
| ⌐ | 0000101 | ▪ | 1100110 |
| ● | 0001101 | L | 1101110 |
| — | 0010101 | ¬ | 1110110 |
| ♣ | 0011101 | — | 1111110 |